BIG SISTER BLUES

WRITTEN BY KIMMIA M. FELDER
ALICEN FELDER AND DR. KELLI FELDER
ILLUSTRATED BY LEENA SHARIQ

© Copyright 2020,

KimMia M. Felder,
Alicen Felder and Dr. Kelli Felder

All rights reserved.
No part of this book may be used or reproduced by any means, graphic, electronic, or mechanical, including photocopying, recording, taping or by any information storage retrieval system without the written permission of the publisher except in the case of brief quotations embodied in critical articles and reviews.

ISBN: 978-1-7350450-0-9

It's not easy being your parent's oldest child, and if you have a little sister like I do then you know all about the Big Sister Blues. My name is KimMia and the first 3 ½ years of my life were the best. I had mom and dad all to myself. It was all about, Me, Me, Me. Then it happened, my little sister Apple was born. The me became smaller and smaller, and suddenly it was always we, we, we; that's right my little sister and me.

You see before my little sister Apple was born, I got everyone's attention, but then everyone wanted to see, hold, and bring things for the new baby. They forgot all about me.

At first everyone coming to see Apple was okay with me, I still had my own friends, my own room, and my own activities. I knew my parents loved me, but now I had to share them and all of my things with my little sister.

My room became our room, my friends became our friends, and my activities became our activities. She wanted everything I had.

When Apple was very little, I liked helping to feed her, teach her, and even play with her. I told my parents; I had to draw the line and would not help change her diapers. She ate way too much fiber for me!

After Apple's 5th birthday, she went from being my cute little sister, to a pesky little tag-a-long. She wanted to go everywhere I was going and do everything I was doing, and this is when the big sister blues kicked in for me.

Whenever mom bought something for me, Apple wanted it too. One day I noticed everything I had she had, and we were dressing alike too. I loved my little sister, but I did not want to look like her every day! We wore the same Easter dresses, Halloween costumes, track suits, leggings, hair ribbons, boots, and raincoats too.

Apple was in my choir, acting and karate classes. She was on my cheer and soccer teams too. I could not escape her. Even though we shared the same room, I found myself sharing my bed too. In the middle of the night, Apple would get out of her bed and come and sleep in my bed with me. She hogged the pillows, sheets, and would kick me all night.

I told my mom, "I have had enough, this must stop!"
"Mom, Apple is taking over everything; my style, my friends, my head, and now my very own bed!"
My mom explained to me that Apple copies me because she loves me. Mom said, "Apple thinks you're awesome."
 Everything you do Apple wants to do too. "Imitation is the best form of flattery", mom said.

I had to think about my conversation with mom for a long time and it finally sunk in. I thought about tennis pros Venus and her little sister Serena, singers Beyoncé and her sister Solange, as well as Chloe and her sister Halle, and then me and my sister Apple.

My sister is great because I am great! I made a path for myself and Apple is simply travelling the same road. I thought about how I help Apple with soccer, school assignments, speeches, choir songs and anything else she needs.

I know Apple copies me because she admires me and loves me, so I am no longer angry about her following me and wanting to dress like me.

I have outgrown the big sister blues, because I now have the big sister luxury of helping my little sister be the best she can be, just like me.

The End

Real Life Sisters

KimMia is a humble 15-year-old high school student that enjoys staying active. She has been a member of several sporting teams; soccer, volleyball, basketball, softball, karate, cheering and swimming. Her current favorite pastimes include writing, singing, dancing, cheering and listening to music. She has written several colorful stories since primary school and finally decided to share one of her literary works with the world. KimMia loves to sing and has sung in various choirs since the age of three. She is currently singing with her church choir, school choir and the world-renowned Detroit Youth Choir. In addition to writing more books, her future aspirations are to pursue a career in music.

"Apple" is the nickname of KimMia's younger sister Alicen Marie. Alicen is a 12-year-old student, author, spoken word artist and actress. She shares many interests with KimMia and also singing in the choir, plays basketball, soccer, swims, and loves to dance. Alicen has also written a book; Say A Little Prayer that released in February 2020. In addition to writing, Apple has performed oral recitations across the country since she was 6 years old. She also enjoys acting and has appeared in a television commercial, stage plays, a short independent film, on live television and in a music video. Apple's current dream is to be a professional soccer player.

www.ingramcontent.com/pod-product-compliance
Lightning Source LLC
Chambersburg PA
CBHW061235070526
44584CB00030B/4137